MW01248280

Greetings from DELAND FLA.

Home of STETSON UNIVERSITY

Greetings from DELAND FLA.

Home of
STETSON UNIVERSITY

Greetings from DeLAND FLA.
Home of
STETSON UNIVERSITY

Printed in the USA
CPSIA information can be obtained
at www.ICGtesting.com
LVHW041235290524
781183LV00006BB/517